AHAA

Diese Buchreihe versammelt die Bauwerke einzelner, mit hohem Qualitätsanspruch ausgewählter jüngerer Schweizer Architekten. Seit 2004 kuratiere ich die Reihe *Anthologie* in der Form einfacher Werkdokumentationen. Sie ist vergleichbar mit der «Blütenlese», wie sie in der Literatur für eine Sammlung ausgewählter Texte angewendet wird. Es liegt in der Natur des Architektenberufs, dass die Erstlingswerke junger Architekten meist kleinere übersichtliche Bauaufgaben sind. Sie sind eine Art Fingerübung, mit der sie das Erlernte anwenden und ihr architektonisches Sensorium erproben und entfalten können. Die Begabung und die Leidenschaft für das Metier lassen sich dabei früh in voller Deutlichkeit und Frische erkennen. So stecken in jedem der kleinen und grossen Projekte inspirierte Grundgedanken und Vorstellungen, die spielerisch und gleichermassen perfekt in architektonische Bilder, Formen und Räume umgesetzt werden. Damit wird mir wieder einmal bewusst, dass in der Architektur wie in anderen Kunstformen die Bilder und Ideen, die hinter dem Werk stehen, das Wesentliche sind. Es mag diese Intuition sein, die der Künstler hat, und die dann über sein Werk wie ein Funke auf den Betrachter überspringt, so wie es der italienische Philosoph Benedetto Croce in seinen Schriften eindringlich beschreibt.

Heinz Wirz
Verleger

This book series presents buildings by selected young Swiss architects that set themselves high quality standards. Since 2004, I have been curating the *Anthologie* series by simply documenting their oeuvre. The series can be compared to a literary anthology presenting a collection of selected texts. It is in the nature of the architectural profession that early works by young architects are mostly small, limited building tasks. They are a kind of five-finger exercise in which the architects apply what they have learnt, as well as testing and developing their architectural instincts. Talent and a passion for the profession can be seen at an early stage in all of its clarity and freshness. Each project, be it large or small, contains an inspired underlying concept and ideas that are playfully and consummately implemented as architectural images, forms and spaces. Thus, I am regularly reminded that in architecture, as in other art forms, the images and ideas behind the works are their essence. Perhaps this is the same intuition described so vividly by the Italian philosopher Benedetto Croce, one that is absorbed by the artist and flies like a spark via the work to the viewer.

Heinz Wirz
Publisher

AHAA

QUART

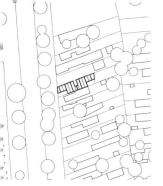

HAUS MIT DREI HÖFEN, GALATI, RUMÄNIEN
2010–2013

Das bestehende «Waggonhaus» auf einer für Rumänien typischen langen und schmalen Parzelle ist durch die traditionelle Aneinanderreihung von Zimmern über Generationen hinweg entstanden. Wie bei vielen Häusern dieser Art entsprach es in keiner Weise mehr den aktuellen Nutzungsanforderungen und drohte, verlassen oder abgerissen zu werden. Durch eine einfache, aber radikale architektonische Geste konnten zwei Grundprobleme gelöst und den Bewohnern ein Weiterleben in ihrem historischen Umfeld ermöglicht werden. Durch das seitliche Einfügen eines langen Wohnraums und das gleichzeitige Umwandeln eines bestehenden Raums in den zentralen Hof kann jedes Zimmer sowohl direkt erschlossen, als auch über einen jeweils vorgelagerten intimen Hof belichtet werden. Kleine Giebeldächer ersetzen das undichte Dach und zeichnen die ursprünglichen Zellen des Hauses nach. Der neue Wohnraum wächst so gleichsam aus dem Bestand hervor und erhält gleichzeitig seinen sehr eigenen Charakter. Die Gebäudeform und die im lokalen Kombinat hergestellte Zinkblechverkleidung erinnern an Lagerhäuser oder Werkstätten und sind eine ironische Anspielung auf zahlreiche parasitäre Nutzungen, mit denen die Wohnquartiere in der Stadt zu kämpfen haben.

Holzbau: Holz & Stein, Gernot Prade, Sibiu (Hermannstadt), RO
HLKS: HAM Tehnic, Andrei Handolescu, Bukarest, RO
Schreiner: Samuel Prest, Radu Suteu, Tulcea, RO

Timber construction: Holz & Stein, Gernot Prade, Sibiu, RO
HVAC: HAM Tehnic, Andrei Handolescu, Bucharest, RO
Carpenter: Samuel Prest, Radu Suteu, Tulcea, RO

HOUSE WITH THREE COURTYARDS, GALATI, ROMANIA
2010–2013

The existing "wagon house" on a classic long and narrow plot of land that is typical for Romania had developed over generations through the traditional sequence of rooms one after the other. Like many others of its kind, it no longer met the current usage requirements in any way and was to be demolished or abandoned. The structural fabric of the building was to be largely preserved to allow the residents to continue living in a home steeped in history. The two basic problems of this type, lighting and access to every room, are solved by a simple but radical architectural gesture. By adding a long living room on the side and transforming one indoor room into a central outdoor space, every room gains direct access and is lit naturally through an intimate courtyard. Small gable roofs replace the unsound roof and trace the outline of the house's original cells. As a result, the new living space emerges from the existing structure and is given its own unique character at the same time. The building shape and homogeneous metal envelope are reminiscent of a warehouse or commercial buildings and an ironic play on the many parasitic uses that the city's living quarters have to battle with.

10 m

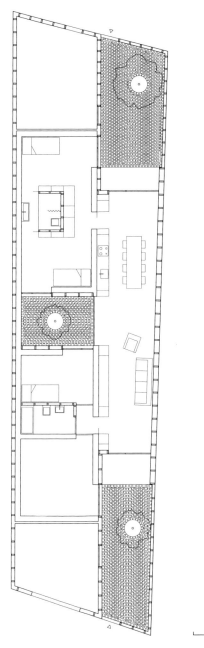

5 m

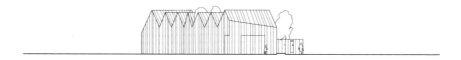

10 m

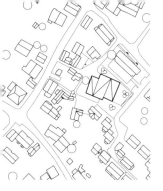

COLLÈGE DE LA ROMANELLAZ, CRISSIER
2012–2016

Das neue Primarschulhaus befindet sich im Zentrum von Crissier. Die Aussicht ist nach allen Seiten hin attraktiv und die Schüler kommen aus allen vier Himmelsrichtungen. Das Gebäude hat folglich keine spezifische Ausrichtung und kann von zwei Seiten aus auf unterschiedlichen Niveaus betreten werden. Zwei Einschnitte und mehrere Dachknicke gliedern das relativ grosse Bauvolumen und binden es zugleich in das kleinmassstäbliche Umfeld des historischen Dorfkerns ein. Die Schule organisiert sich um eine zweiläufige zentrale Treppe, welche als identitätsstiftendes Element alle vier Geschosse miteinander verbindet und im Brandfall die Entfluchtung über zwei separate Brandabschnitte ermöglicht. Obwohl das Gebäude zu grossen Teilen unter der Erde liegt, sind alle Schulzimmer zweiseitig und die Turnhalle sogar dreiseitig belichtet.

Bauingenieur: Muttoni
Fernández, Ecublens
Lichtkunst: Atelier Daniel
Schläpfer, Lausanne

**Civil engineer: Muttoni
Fernández, Ecublens
Lighting art: Atelier Daniel
Schläpfer, Lausanne**

ROMANELLAZ PRIMARY SCHOOL, CRISSIER
2012–2016

The new primary school is situated in the middle of the village. The children come from all directions and the view on all sides is exciting. Consequently, the building does not have a specific orientation and can be entered from two sides on two different levels. The large construction volume is integrated into the small-scale setting by two recesses and several bends in the roof, forcing itself into the tight building perimeter, directly adjacent to the historical village centre. The school is organised around a double central staircase, which is the unifying element that links all four floors to each other, while also providing emergency escape routes via two separate fire compartments in the event of a fire. Although large parts of the building are sunken, all classrooms are lit from two sides, the gym even from three.

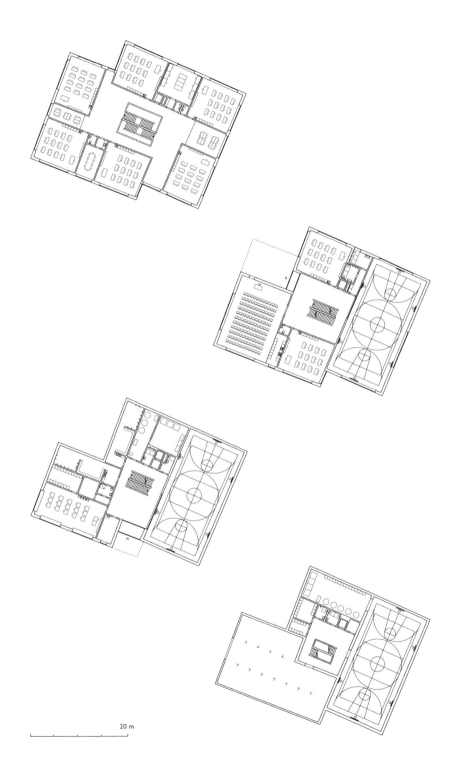

20 m

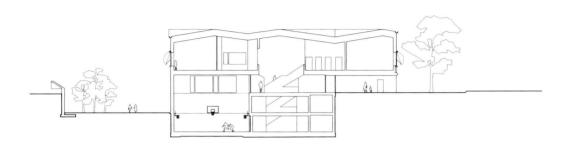

10 m

WOHNEN UNTER DEM DACH, BUKAREST, RUMÄNIEN
2011–2013

In vielen rumänischen Wohngebäuden bleibt der Raum unter dem Dach ohne Funktion, da feuerpolizeiliche Richtlinien keine Nutzung zulassen. So auch in diesem Wohnblock aus der Zeit zwischen den beiden Weltkkriegen, in dem die Wohnung im obersten Geschoss mit ihrer zellulären Struktur für den Bewohner zu eng wurde. Der Umbau stellt vielfältige visuelle Beziehungen her, um innerhalb der engen physischen Grenzen eine Wirkung der Grosszügigkeit zu erreichen. Wohn- und Essbereich umgeben eine nach innen erweiterte Terrasse; das frei stehende Küchenmöbel trennt sie, ohne den visuellen Bezug zu kappen. Die sanitären Funktionen sind aufgeteilt, um den gleichzeitigen Gebrauch von mehreren Personen zu ermöglichen. Durch die Einführung der dritten Dimension entsteht ein erstaunlicher räumlicher Reichtum. Eine vormals dunkle Ecke wird dank der Öffnung nach oben zum Zentrum der Wohnung. Der Umbau entzieht sich den üblichen mit Mansardenwohnungen verbundenen Klischees, da der Dachraum nur fragmentarisch integriert wird, um so punktuell vertikale Akzente zu setzten. Wie der Bewohner hat die Wohnung etwas Kosmopolitisch-Exzentrisches, bleibt aber zugleich bescheiden und geerdet.

Holzbau: Holz & Stein,
Gernot Prade, Sibiu
(Hermannstadt), RO
HLKS: HAM Tehnic, Andrei
Handolescu, Bukarest, RO
Schreiner: Radu Proteasa,
Valcea, RO

**Timber construction: Holz
& Stein, Gernot Prade,
Sibiu, RO
HVAC: HAM Tehnic, Andrei
Handolescu, Bucharest, RO
Carpenter: Radu Proteasa,
Valcea, RO**

UNDER THE ATTIC, BUCHAREST, ROMANIA
2011–2013

The space under the pitched roof is left unused in most Romanian residential buildings as fire safety regulations do not permit its use. Thus, a great deal of potential space is left unexploited. This is also the case in this interwar-period housing block where the young owner outgrew the apartment on the top floor with its cellular structure. To create a feeling of spaciousness within the tight confinements, the project establishes various visual relationships in particular by breaking up the sanitary functions. The living and dining areas surround a previously barely usable terrace that is extended inwards; the free-standing kitchen furniture divides it without obstructing the visual reference. An astonishing abundance of space is created by introducing a third dimension. A previously dark, unattractive corner becomes the spatial heart of the apartment thanks to the skylight. The project evades the usual clichés associated with attic apartments as the roof space is only integrated in a fragmentary way to create occasional vertical accentuation. Like the resident, the apartment has an eccentrically cosmopolitan character, while remaining modestly down-to-earth.

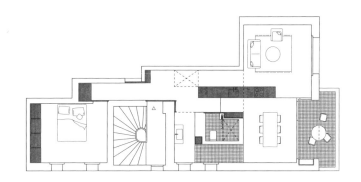

5 m

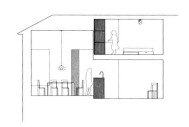

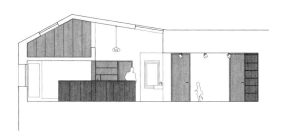

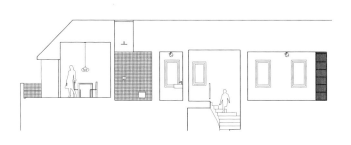

5 m

24

DIENSTWOHNUNGEN FÜR GRENZWACHTKORPS, VERNIER
2014–2020

Landschaft: Weber +
Brönnimann, Bern

**Landscaping: Weber +
Brönnimann, Bern**

Der Neubau mit 32 Wohnungen befindet sich am Stadtrand Genfs auf einem leicht geneigten Südhang. Das Gebäude bewohnen Mitarbeiter des Grenzwachtkorps mit einem unregelmässigen Tagesablauf und ihre Familien. Die Lärmbelastung durch die Nähe zur Autobahn und zur Anflugschneise des Flughafens steht daher hohen nutzerspezifischen Schallschutzanforderungen gegenüber. Die spezielle Grundrissform des Neubaus entwickelt sich aus dieser Problematik heraus, ausgehend von der einzelnen Wohnung, deren Wohnraum jeweils nach zwei oder drei Seiten ausgerichtet ist. Der Bewohner erhält so den Vorteil, wählen zu können, wohin er sich orientieren möchte. Das polygonale Volumen vermeidet es, den Bestandsgebäuden den Rücken zuzuwenden und bindet diese in die neue Logik der gemeinschaftlichen Aussenräume ein. Der organisch anmutende Grundriss wirkt auf den ersten Blick ungeordnet, er ist jedoch durchaus rational aufgebaut und bedient sich lediglich zweier unterschiedlicher Winkel.

HOUSING UNITS FOR BORDER GUARDS, VERNIER
2014–2020

The new building with 32 apartments is situated on the outskirts of Geneva on a gentle south-facing slope. The building is inhabited by customs officers with an irregular daily routine and their families. The noise pollution due to its proximity to the motorway and airport faces high user-specific noise control requirements. The new building's special floor plan responds to this issue, based on an individual apartment with a living area facing two or three sides. Thus the residents always have the psychological advantage of choosing the direction in which they wish to orientate themselves. The polygonal building volume avoids turning its back on the existing buildings and integrates them into the new logic of the communal outdoor spaces. The seemingly organic floor plan looks wild at first glance, but in fact has an extremely rational structure and only uses two angles.

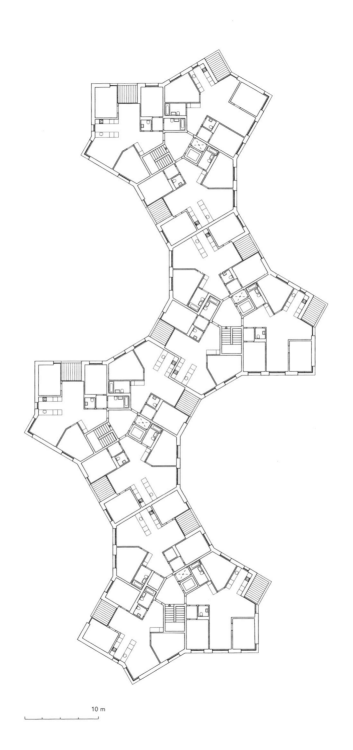

10 m

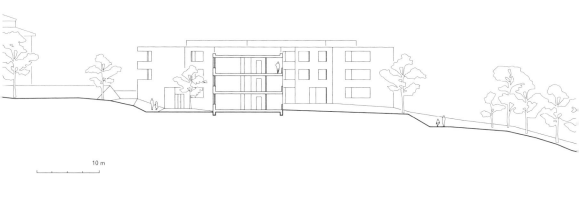

10 m

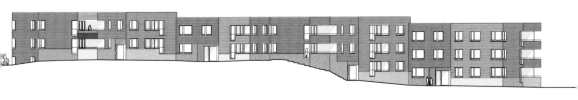

10 m

ALTERS- UND PFLEGEHEIM AESCHEN, AMDEN
2017, Selektiver Projektwettbewerb, 2. Preis

Das neue Pflegeheim liegt oberhalb des Alpendorfs Amden an einem grünen Hang. Dieser fällt südseitig steil zum Walensee ab und steigt nordseitig ebenso steil zum Mattstock an. Die Wahrnehmung der Bewohner ist bestimmt durch den Hausberg und das Panorama. Das Gebäude sitzt im Hang wie ein scharfkantiger Fels. Seine Form hat ihren Ursprung in der Topografie des Geländes, aus dem es hervorzuwachsen scheint, und dem Panorama, dem es sich öffnet. Der Grundriss der Pflegestationen versucht die Vorteile eines einbündigen Längsbaus und eines mehrseitig orientierten Punkthauses zu vereinen. Während alle Zimmer von der überwältigenden Aussicht in die Bergwelt profitieren, entsteht in den gemeinschaftlich genutzten Bereichen eine abwechslungsreiche Raumwelt mit vielfältigen Bezügen zur nahen und fernen Umgebung.

AESCHEN NURSING HOME, AMDEN
2017, Selective project competition, 2nd Prize

The new nursing home is situated above the Alpine village of Amden on a green slope. On the south side, it drops steeply towards the lake, while on the north side it rises steeply towards the mountain, which combines with the panorama to dominate one's perception. The building sits on the slope like a jagged rock. Its shape originates from the topography of the terrain it is growing out of and the panorama it opens up to. The floor plan of the nursing ward tries to marry the benefits of a single-winged longitudinal building and a multilaterally oriented point block. The residents' rooms all face the overwhelming view of the mountain panorama, while a diverse interior landscape emerges in the communal areas, offering manifold vistas of the nearby and distant surroundings.

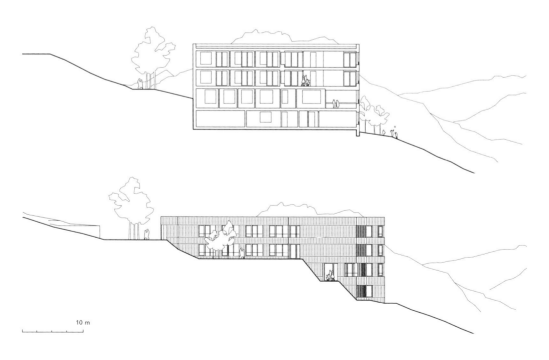

10 m

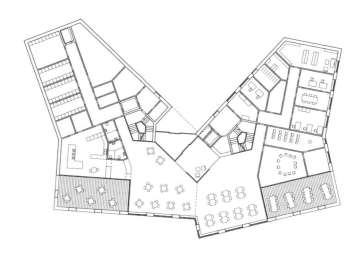

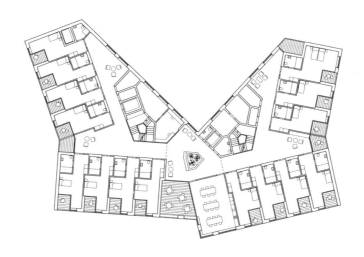

10 m

ERWEITERUNG SCHULANLAGE GRENTSCHEL, LYSS
2018–2021

Landschaft: Weber +
Brönnimann, Bern
Holzbau-Ingenieur: Makiol
Wiederkehr, Beinwil
Klangkunst: Studio Zimoun,
Bern

**Landscaping: Weber +
Brönnimann, Bern
Timber construction
engineer: Makiol
Wiederkehr, Beinwil
Sound art: Studio Zimoun,
Bern**

Die grossmasstäblichen Gebäude im Grentschel erscheinen auf den ersten Blick wie zufällig über die Talsohle verstreut. Tatsächlich spielt der unschein-bare Grentschelbach jedoch eine ordnende Rolle. Alle Gebäudevolumina sind zum Bachlauf ausgerichtet und stehen jeweils parallel dazu. Das Projekt fügt sich in diese Logik ein, wobei ein entspanntes Ensemble mit fliessenden Aussen-räumen entsteht. Im Zentrum des Areals entsteht ein zweigeschossiger Bau, in dem die gemeinschaftlich genutzten Funktionen Aula, Bibliothek und Tages-schule vereint sind. Der bestehende trapezförmige Pausenplatz wird durch einen wesensgleichen gespiegelten ergänzt. Im Osten sind im neuen Schulhaus über drei Geschosse die Unterrichtsräume untergebracht. Sie sind alle zwei-seitig übereck belichtet und haben über die raumhohen Fenster einen starken Aussenraumbezug. Die stringente, geradlinige Fassadenkonstruktion erhält durch alternierende schalungsglatte und sandgestrahlte Oberflächenbereiche einen beinahe verspielten Ausdruck. Der dabei entstehende «effet Tromp-l'Œil» suggeriert eine Tiefe, die in Wirklichkeit nicht existiert, und verleiht den Ge-bäuden eine leichte, klassisch-elegante Erscheinung im Kontast zu der wild-romantischen Landschaft des Grentschelbachs.

GRENTSCHEL SCHOOL EXTENSION, LYSS
2018–2021

At first glance, the large buildings in Grentschel appear to be randomly scattered across the valley floor. However, the unassuming Grentschel stream actually plays an organising role. Each building volume is orien-tated towards the course of the stream and positioned parallel to it. The project adopts this logic, resulting in a relaxed ensemble with fluent outdoor spaces. At the centre of the campus, a two-storey construction houses the collective spaces – assembly hall, library and day school. The existing trapezoidal school yard is complemented by a second identical but mirrored square, perpetuating this spacial peculiarity. To the east, the new school building houses the classrooms. They all benefit from floor-to-ceiling windows on two sides that incorporate the green out-doors. With its alternating smooth and sandblasted surfaces, the simple and rigorous façade is given an almost playful appearance. The provoked tromp l'oeil effect suggests a depth that does not really exist and gives the buildings a light, classically elegant appearance, which contrasts with the wild romantic landscape of the Grentschel stream.

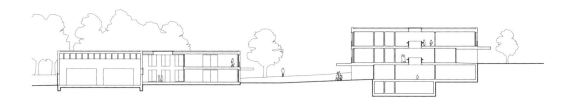

20 m

20 m

ANDREAS HEIERLE

1982	geboren in Schwyz
1988–2001	Schulen in Steinen, Schwyz und Bangkok (TH)
2002–2008	Architekturstudium an der AAM, Accademia di Architettura di Mendrisio
2004–2005	Praktikum bei NMBW architecture studio, Melbourne (AU)
2005–2006	Austauschjahr an der ENSA, Marseille (FR)
2008–2011	Mitarbeit bei Lussi + Halter Architekten, Luzern
2010–2012	Zusammenarbeit mit Cristina Trofin an Projekten in Rumänien
2012	Gründung ahaa, Andreas Heierle Atelier für Architektur

CRISTINA TROFIN

1980	geboren in Tulcea (RO)
2000–2007	Architekturstudium an der Universität Ion Mincu, Bucharest (RO) und der ENSA, Marseille (FR)
2006	Praktikum bei Lévy Magnan Architectes, Marseille (FR)
2008–2009	Mitarbeit bei Christ & Gantenbein, Basel
2009–2010	Mitarbeit bei Zimmermann Architekten, Aarau
2010–2014	Zusammenarbeit mit Andreas Heierle an Projekten in Rumänien
2011–2015	Mitarbeit bei Scheitlin Syfrig Architekten, Luzern
2015–2019	Partnerin bei ahaa

MITARBEITENDE
(* aktuell)

Carligianu Andi, Jasper Andresen, Melanie Bareither*, Mengxing Cao, Daniel Carvalho*, Elena Ifrim, Naznin Parvin, Barbara Romanska, Michael Roth*, Sara Sali*, Zeljko Savic, Jean-Michael Taillebois, Joan Albert Tolrà Campanyà*, Cristina Trofin*

ANDREAS HEIERLE

1982	Born in Schwyz
2002–2008	Studied Architecture at the AAM, Accademia di Architettura di Mendrisio
2004–2005	Internship at NMBW architecture studio, Melbourne (AU)
2005–2006	Exchange year at ENSA, Marseille (FR)
2008–2011	Employed at Lussi + Halter Architekten, Lucerne
2010–2012	Collaboration with Cristina Trofin on projects in Romania
2012	Founded ahaa, Andreas Heierle Atelier für Architektur

CRISTINA TROFIN

1980	Born in Tulcea (RO)
2000-2007	Studied Architecture at the "Ion Mincu" University of Architecture and Urban Planning, Bucharest (RO) and ENSA, Marseille (FR)
2006	Internship at Lévy Magnan Architectes, Marseille (FR)
2008–2009	Employed at Christ & Gantenbein, Basel
2009–2010	Employed at Zimmermann Architekten, Aarau
2010–2014	Collaboration with Andreas Heierle on projects in Romania
2011–2015	Employed at Scheitlin Syfrig Architekten, Lucerne
2015–2019	Partner at ahaa

EMPLOYEES
(* current)   Carligianu Andi, Jasper Andresen, Melanie Bareither*, Mengxing Cao, Daniel Carvalho*, Elena Ifrim, Naznin Parvin, Barbara Romanska, Michael Roth*, Sara Sali*, Zeljko Savic, Jean-Michael Taillebois, Joan Albert Tolrà Campanyà*, Cristina Trofin*

WERKVERZEICHNIS (AUSWAHL)

2013	Haus mit drei Höfen, Galati (RO)
	Um- und Ausbau Dachwohnung, Bukarest (RO)
2014	Selektiver Projektwettbewerb, Umnutzung und
	Erweiterung Schulanlage Räfis, Buchs; 2. Rang
2015	Selektiver Projektwettbewerb, Altersheim Erlenhaus,
	Engelberg; 3. Rang
2016	Collège de la Romanellaz, Crissier; offener Projekt-
	wettbewerb 2012; 1. Rang; in Zusammenarbeit mit
	Daniel Willi
2017	Offener Projektwettbewerb, Nationales Schwimmsport-
	zentrum, Tenero; 5. Rang
	Selektiver Projektwettbewerb, Erweiterung Altersheim,
	Büren an der Aare; 4. Rang
	Selektiver Projektwettbewerb, Erweiterung Schulanlage
	Gestadeck, Liestal; 4. Rang
	Selektiver Projektwettbewerb, Alters- und Pflegeheim
	Aeschen, Amden; 2. Rang
2018	Selektiver Projektwettbewerb, Plegezentrum Du Lac,
	St. Moritz; 2. Rang
	Eingeladener Projektwettbewerb, Entwicklung
	Industriestrassen-Quartier, Luzern; 5. Rang
2019	Selektiver Projektwettbewerb, Primarschule Wiesental,
	Baar; 3. Rang
	Selektiver Projektwettbewerb, Erweiterung Schulanlage
	Altikofen, Ittigen; 3. Rang
	Selektiver Projektwettbewerb, Wohnüberbauung
	Stöcklimatt, Hitzkirch; 3. Rang
2020	Dienstwohnungen für Grenzwachtkorps, Vernier; offener
	Projektwettbewerb 2014; 1. Rang

Laufende Projekte

2018–	Erweiterung Schulanlage Grentschel, Lyss; selektiver
	Projektwettbewerb 2018; 1. Rang
2019–	Lupulesti Retreat, Vaideeni (RO)
2020–	Mehrfamilienhäuser Dreilinden, Mettmenstetten;
	Studienauftrag 2020, 1. Rang

BIBLIOGRAFIE

2013	Andreas Heierle, Cristina Trofin: The wagon-house with
	seven roofs. In: Zeppelin, Nr. 110, Bukarest (RO)
	The Small and Generous Loft. In: Zeppelin, Nr. 122,
	Bukarest (RO)
	ahaa – La curte. In: Case din Romania 5, Igloo, Bukarest (RO)
	ahaa – La Curte. In: Arhitectura Romaneasca in detalii
	– Transformari, Editura Ozalid, Bukarest (RO)
2017	Centro sportivo nazionale di nuoto, Tenero.
	In: Hochparterre Wettbewerbe Nr. 03, Zürich
	Erweiterung Primarschule Gestadeck, Liestal.
	In: Hochparterre Wettbewerbe Nr. 04, Zürich
2018	Entwicklung Areal Industriestrasse, Luzern.
	In: Hochparterre Wettbewerbe Nr. 04, Zürich
2019	Neubau Schule Wiesental, Baar. In: Hochparterre
	Wettbewerbe Nr. 01, Zürich
2020	Mehrgenerationenquartier Stöcklimatt, Hitzkirch.
	In: Hochparterre Wettbewerbe Nr. 03, Zürich

LIST OF WORKS (SELECTION)

2013	House with three courtyards, Galati (RO)
	Attic apartment conversion and extension, Bucharest (RO)
2014	Selective project competition, Räfis School conversion and extension, Buchs; 2nd Prize
2015	Selective project competition, Erlenhaus home for the elderly, Engelberg; 3rd Prize
2016	Collège de la Romanellaz, Crissier; open project competition in 2012; 1st Prize; in collaboration with Daniel Willi
2017	Open project competition, National Swimming Sports Centre, Tenero; 5th Prize
	Selective project competition, extension, home for the elderly, Büren an der Aare; 4th Prize
	Selective project competition, Gestadeck School extension, Liestal; 4th Prize
	Selective project competition, Aeschen home and nursing centre for the elderly, Amden; 2nd Prize
2018	Selective project competition, Du Lac nursing centre for the elderly, St. Moritz; 2nd Prize
	Invited project competition, Industriestrasse neighbourhood development, Lucerne; 5th Prize
2019	Selective project competition, Wiesental Primary School, Baar; 3rd Prize
	Selective project competition, Altikofen School extension, Ittigen; 3rd Prize
	Selective project competition, Stöcklimatt housing development, Hitzkirch; 3rd Prize
2020	Official lodgings, Border Guard Corps, Vernier; open project competition in 2014; 1st Prize

	Current projects
2018–	Grentschel School extension, Lyss; selective project competition in 2018, 1st Prize
2019–	Lupulesti Retreat, Vaideeni (RO)
2020–	Dreilinden Residential buildings, Mettmenstetten; invited project competition 2020, 1st Prize

BIBLIOGRAPHY

2013	Andreas Heierle, Cristina Trofin: "The wagon-house with seven roofs". In: *Zeppelin*, No. 110, Bucharest (RO)
	"The Small and Generous Loft". In: *Zeppelin*, No. 122, Bucharest (RO)
	"ahaa – La curte". In: *Case din Romania* 5, Igloo, Bucharest (RO)
	"ahaa – La Curte". In: *Arhitectura Romaneasca in detalii – Transformari*, Editura Ozalid, Bucharest (RO)
2017	"Centro sportivo nazionale di nuoto, Tenero". In: *Hochparterre Wettbewerbe* No. 03, Zurich
	"Erweiterung Primarschule Gestadeck, Liestal". In: *Hochparterre Wettbewerbe* No. 04, Zurich
2018	"Entwicklung Areal Industriestrasse, Luzern". In: *Hochparterre Wettbewerbe* No. 04, Zurich
2019	"Neubau Schule Wiesental, Baar". In: *Hochparterre Wettbewerbe* No. 01, Zurich
2020	"Mehrgenerationenquartier Stöcklimatt, Hitzkirch". In: *Hochparterre Wettbewerbe* No. 03, Zurich

ahaa
46. Band der Reihe Anthologie
Herausgeber: Heinz Wirz, Luzern
Konzept: Heinz Wirz; ahaa, Luzern
Projektleitung: Quart Verlag, Antonia Chavez-Wirz
Textlektorat Deutsch: Kirsten Rachowiak, München DE
Übersetzung Deutsch–Englisch: Benjamin Liebelt, Berlin DE
Textlektorat Englisch: Benjamin Liebelt, Berlin DE
Fotos: Andrei Margulescu, Bukarest RO S. 7–25, Stefan Zürrer,
Buchrain S. 27–33
Visualisierungen: MOTIV, Gdynia PL S. 35–36, ONIRISM,
Mailand IT S. 39–41
Redesign: BKVK, Basel – Beat Keusch, Angelina Köpplin-Stützle
Grafische Umsetzung: Quart Verlag
Lithos: Printeria, Luzern
Druck: DZA Druckerei zu Altenburg GmbH, Altenburg

ahaa
Volume 46 of the series Anthologie
Edited by: Heinz Wirz, Lucerne
Concept: Heinz Wirz; ahaa, Lucerne
Project management: Quart Verlag, Antonia Chavez-Wirz
German text editing: Kirsten Rachowiak, Munich DE
German–English translation: Benjamin Liebelt, Berlin DE
English text editing: Benjamin Liebelt, Berlin DE
Photos: Andrei Margulescu, Bucharest RO p. 7–25,
Stefan Zürrer, Buchrain p. 27–33
Visualisation: MOTIV, Gdynia PL p. 35–36, ONIRISM,
Milan IT p. 39–41
Redesign: BKVK, Basel – Beat Keusch,
Angelina Köpplin-Stützle
Graphical layout: Quart Verlag
Lithos: Printeria, Lucerne
Printing: DZA Druckerei zu Altenburg GmbH, Altenburg

ERNST GÖHNER STIFTUNG

Schweizerische Eidgenossenschaft
Confédération suisse
Confederazione Svizzera
Confederaziun svizra

Eidgenössisches Departement des Innern EDI
Bundesamt für Kultur BAK

Quart Verlag GmbH
Denkmalstrasse 2, CH-6006 Luzern
books@quart.ch, www.quart.ch

books@quart.ch, www.quart.ch